SPIRITUAL READINESS

Stephen Kaung

ISBN: 978-1-942521-56-3

Available from:

Christian Testimony Ministry
4424 Huguenot Road
Richmond, Virginia 23235

www.christiantestimonyministry.com

Printed in USA

CONTENTS

Preface 1

Why Must We Be Ready? 3

How Can We Be Ready? 31

Questions & Answers 59

PREFACE

The following ministry was given by Brother Stephen Kaung at the Northeast Christian Weekend Conference, in October 2006. The theme for the conference was *Spiritual Readiness.* The conference concluded with a question and answer period, which is included as the last chapter.

The spoken messages have been transcribed into this booklet with minimal editing done for clarity, while maintaining the spoken form.

For love's sake, may we as God's people be spiritually ready for the coming of the Lord in our hearts and spirits.

Christian Testimony Ministry

WHY MUST WE BE READY?

Matthew 24:32-45—But learn the parable from the fig-tree: When already its branch becomes tender and produces leaves, ye know that the summer is near. Thus also ye, when ye see all these things, know that it is near, at the doors. Verily I say to you, This generation will not have passed away until all these things shall have taken place. The heaven and the earth shall pass away, but my words shall in no wise pass away. But of that day and hour no one knows, not even the angels of the heavens, but my Father alone. But as the days of Noah, so also shall be the coming of the Son of man. For as they were in the days which were before the flood, eating and drinking, marrying and giving in marriage, until the day on which Noah entered into the ark, and they knew not till the flood came and took all away; thus also shall be the coming of the Son of man. Then two shall be in the field, one is taken and one is left; two women grinding at the mill, one is taken and one is left. Watch therefore, for ye know not in what hour your Lord comes. But know this, that if the master of the house had known in what watch the thief was coming, he would have watched and not have suffered his house to be dug through into. Wherefore ye also, be ye ready, for in that hour that ye think not the Son of man comes. Who then is the faithful and prudent bondman whom his lord has set over his household, to give them food in season?

The song, "Since Long Ago at Bethany We Parted," always touches me very deeply. This was a song written by our dear brother Watchman Nee during the persecution in China. He wrote this song to express not only his own feeling but also the feeling of all the saints throughout the generations. And hopefully this same feeling will be in each one of us. The more we look into what is going on in the world, the greater the cry of our heart: "Oh Lord, how long?" Generation after generation, believers, true believers, those who love the Lord have been waiting for the long promise of His return. But somehow He is delayed.

We remember what Peter said, "To God, a day is like a thousand years and a thousand years is like one day." It is not that our Lord delays His return; it is because of His longsuffering. How He suffers long for His own bride! As long as His bride is not ready He has nothing to come to, to return to. So how important it is, not for ourselves but for our beloved Lord, that we be ready. He will not delay even a moment if His bride is made ready. So this is the reason why we gather together this time. I do feel the importance of this hour. Everything seems to indicate to us that His return is imminent. We cannot go on; the world cannot go on any longer. Every sign shows that His return is very near. And may we be a generation that has the privilege of welcoming Him in our time. And I hope that this will be the prayer of our hearts.

Let's have a word of prayer:

Dear Lord, we do praise and thank Thee for gathering us together here this time. We thank Thee for Thy longsuffering. We thank Thee for Thy lovingkindness and tender mercies. Lord, Thou hast created within our heart a longing for Thyself. How much more, Lord, is the longing, the waiting, the desire in Thy heart to come and to receive us to Thyself? Oh dear Lord, do deliver us from being so unwatchful, so complacent. Forgive us for being occupied with so many things that are transient. Lord, do capture our hearts, that there is only one thing in our heart; it is Thou. Oh Lord, use this time to prepare us. We thank Thee that during Thy first coming Thou didst prepare a few here and there whose hearts really prepared the way of Thy coming. Will not Thou, Lord, in these last days also raise up people here, everywhere, throughout the whole world, that will cry unto Thee, "Come quickly, Lord Jesus." Use us to bring back the King. Privilege us, Lord, with this privilege. We offer ourselves once again to Thee. Work in us; prepare us, we ask in Thy precious name. Amen.

I do thank the Lord for the theme of this gathering. I feel that it is not so much having another conference. It is good for us to come together once in a year for fellowship, but I feel this is a very special time. And I thank the Lord that the theme for this time is really timely,

"Spiritual Readiness." When you think of spiritual readiness, probably the first question you will ask is: "Why? Ready for what?" There is nothing more important in the world to be ready for than what we are going to share together. I feel there is only one reason, one and only one reason for spiritual readiness. It is to be ready to welcome the coming of the Lord.

THE LONG PROMISED MESSIAH

From the very beginning of human history, after Adam and Eve sinned, God came to the garden, and He gave man a hope. In Genesis 3:15 it says, "The seed of the woman will crush the serpent's head, and the serpent will crush his heel." This is the promise of God to the sinful world. This is the only way to save and to deliver us. God promised this from the very beginning of human history. And this promise was reiterated, reinforced many, many times throughout the Old Testament through the prophets that God's promise will be fulfilled.

For instance, in Isaiah 9:6-7 it is prophesied: "Unto us a child is born, unto us a son is given; and the government shall be upon his shoulder;

and his name is called Wonderful, Counsellor, Mighty God, Father of Eternity, Prince of Peace. Of the increase of his government and of peace there shall be no end, upon the throne of David and over his kingdom, to establish it, and to uphold it with judgment and with righteousness, from henceforth even for ever. The zeal of Jehovah of hosts will perform this."

At the same time, in Isaiah 53 we have a whole chapter on the coming Messiah, but He will be a suffering One. He will be rejected, and His life will be taken away. He will bear the sin of the world. He will be crushed. Therefore, those in the Old Testament time just could not understand why God promised the seed of the woman to be a reigning One, a glorious One who established His kingdom forever more. Yet at the same time it is prophesied that this Messiah will suffer even unto death. So the Old Testament people were confused. They could not reconcile these two sides of the Messiah. Among the Jews they even questioned whether Isaiah 53 referred to another person because at that time it was not yet revealed. Thank God, He is always faithful to His promise.

After about four thousand years, one day a Child was born of the woman; a Son was given. The Word became flesh. God came to become Man and tabernacled among men, full of grace and truth. Christ had come. But during His lifetime it seemed as if He was interested only in the spiritual condition of His people. He did not seem to be interested in the physical condition of His people. In the beginning the Jewish people welcomed Him, thinking that He might be the long-promised Messiah. But gradually, they lost their faith because He did not seem to be the one that would fulfill all the promises that the government would be upon His shoulder, that He would sit upon the throne of David and rule over the nations.

You remember when our Lord Jesus first began His ministry, He went into the synagogue in Nazareth and they gave Him the scroll of Isaiah. He opened it up and read Isaiah 61: "The Spirit of the Lord is upon Me. He has anointed Me to preach the glad tidings to the poor and to proclaim the acceptable year of the Lord." Then He stopped; He did not finish Isaiah's prophecy. He did not continue on with the day of vengeance. He left something out. Why? It is because in the first coming of our Lord Jesus He is as the Lamb of God who takes away the sin of the world. He is to bear our sins and our sorrow. He is to be our substitute before God. He is to redeem us. That is His work while He was on earth. He left the reigning part, the glorious part, as it were, aside. Instead He said, "The day of My glory" which refers to His crucifixion, not to His enthronement because in the first coming of our Lord He concentrated Himself on the first necessary work. But sometimes, in the Gospels He would try to leak out something in a parable. He did not speak openly and frankly on how He would come back and rule over the nations, but in parables.

THE GOSPELS GIVE HINTS ABOUT HIS RETURN

For instance, in Luke 19 there is the parable of the nobleman. The nobleman went away to receive his kingdom, and before he left he gave ten minas to ten servants and said, "Trade with it until I come." Then one day he came back and he reckoned with his servants. And you know the story—one earned ten more, one earned five, and one was unfaithful. In other words, He did give hints that there would be a returning.

Toward the very last of the time He was on earth, one day as He left Jerusalem His disciples pointed out to Him the beautiful stones that decorated the temple in Jerusalem. The Jews took great pride in this temple; it was so magnificent. But when our Lord left with His disciples from the temple, He quietly said, "Yes, but one day not a stone will be left upon another stone." The temple was built with massive stones, so solid, and yet our Lord said, "One day not a stone upon a stone." The disciples heard it but they dared not say anything on the way because this would be such a shock to the Jews.

But after our Lord arrived on the Mount of Olives, He sat down and four of His disciples came secretly to Him and said, "Lord, Master, when shall these things be, and what will be the sign of Thy coming and the end of this age?" The disciples combined all three things into one. If the temple is destroyed, and completely destroyed, that means the end of the world, and that will be the sign of the coming of the Messiah. But our Lord Jesus began to teach them.

Without going into details probably it will be a help when you read Matthew 24 and 25, the so-called Olivet discourse, to realize that generally speaking, you can divide these two chapters into three sections. The first few verses, of course, are the background. The disciples asked the Lord, "When shall these things be?" When shall the temple be totally destroyed? And then they followed with, "What is the sign of Thy presence and the end of this age?" In answering their questions our Lord seemed to answer towards the three sections of the world—the Jews, the church, and the nations—because the world is composed of the Jews, the church, and the nations. So it seems as if from 24:4-31 this section is addressed especially to the Jews, because if you read carefully you find everything is literal. The Lord does not use parables and everything will be fulfilled literally. Then, in Matthew 24:32—25:30 our Lord addressed the church because there you find parables are being used. It is a spiritual emphasis in that section. The first section is literal, physical; the second section is spiritual in essence. Then of course, the last section in chapter 25:31 onwards to the end is addressed to the nations. If you will remember this, probably it will be a help to your understanding of these two chapters. But do not forget that even though our Lord seemed to be addressing three different people, yet there are many things that overlap and many things that happen to all. So if we remember this, probably it will be a great help.

Even towards the end of the life of our Lord, during His last supper with His disciples, He said, "I go to prepare a place for you, and I will come back and receive you to Myself." When He was judged by the high priest and the Sanhedrin, the high priest, Caiaphas said, "Are you the Son of God?" Our Lord said, "You said it, and you shall see the Son of Man coming on a cloud." So here you find our Lord did hint of His return.

Even in John 21, after His resurrection, He appeared to the seven by the Sea of Tiberias, and He said to Simon Peter, "Come, follow Me." So Peter followed Him, and another disciple also followed. So Peter turned and said to the Lord,

"What about this man?" Of course, he referred to John. And you remember our Lord said, "If I want him to wait until I return what is that to you?" So, even during His first coming, you find hints here and there about His return. He finished the first part of His work, and there is another part He has to finish at His second coming. So today, His second coming is evident to us. There are two comings of Christ, two comings of the Lord. In His first coming He came as the Lamb of God, taking away the sin of the world. But at His second coming He will come as the Lion of Judah, and He will judge the world with righteousness and reign over the world.

THE ASCENSION

If you read Acts 1, you will notice that our Lord Jesus was standing on the Mount of Olives. His disciples were around Him and then He was taken up. He left the Mount of Olives. He ascended and the disciples looked at Him, seeing Him going up until a cloud took Him. They could not see Him anymore, but they were still looking up. At that time two men in white appeared, and they said, "Men of Galilee, why are you looking up? Don't you know that this same Person, Christ, who has been taken up will come back in like manner?" Of course, the disciples saw the Lord going up, but then the cloud took Him and they could not see Him.

Did the Lord really arrive at the throne? Thank God, He did. How do we know? Number one, on the day of Pentecost the Holy Spirit came down from heaven and the hundred and twenty disciples who were waiting in that room were baptized into one body. And that is the evidence that our Lord had arrived at the throne. Why? Because the Bible tells us, and even Peter said it, "What you have seen and heard proves one thing, that God has made Him Lord and Christ." After our Lord Jesus arrived at the throne, then God the Father anointed Him with oil, with the Holy Spirit, and as the oil upon the head of Aaron, it flowed down upon his beard and covered the whole body to the skirt of his garment. That is the picture.

After our Lord was anointed in heaven as the High Priest, then the same oil, the Holy Spirit, came down upon the hundred and twenty, and not only on the hundred and twenty but to the very end of any member in the body of Christ. Glory! That is a definite proof.

Not only that, in Revelation 5, John was in the Spirit and the heaven was opened and he saw a vision. He saw the throne of God, and in the hand of God was a scroll which is the title deed of the universe. Satan may occupy this world as a usurper, but he has never been the owner. The ownership is always in the hand of God. And then John saw a Lamb newly slain, standing; that means resurrection. And the Lamb is the only One who is worthy because He has overcome. He has overcome Satan and all the powers of darkness, and He is worthy to receive that scroll and to open it. Thank God for that. This is a review of the ascension of our Lord Jesus.

So by these two evidences we are sure that our Lord has reached the throne. He is now sitting at the right hand of God waiting for His enemies to be His footstool. If His first coming is true, His second coming must be true.

THE EPISTLES SPEAK OF HIS RETURN

In the Epistles, the writings of the apostles, the return of the Lord, the coming of the Lord is everywhere. For instance, the first epistle in the Bible by the apostle Paul is I Thessalonians. As you read those five chapters, you find the return of the Lord, the coming of the Lord is mentioned in every chapter. In chapter 1 it says that God has saved them, delivered them from idol worshiping to believe in the one true God and to wait for the return of the Son of God. Paul tells the Thessalonians in chapter 2, "You will be my joy and my crown at the coming of the Lord." In chapter 3 he says, "One day the Lord will come with His saints." In chapter 4 it says that the trumpet will sound, the dead in the Lord will be raised, and those who are still living will be changed. And they will be caught up into the air to meet the Lord who has descended from the throne to the air, and they will be with the Lord forever. And in chapter 5 it is the prayer of the apostle Paul for the Thessalonian believers that the God of peace would sanctify them wholly, spirit, soul, and body, and they would be preserved blameless at the coming of the Lord.

In the early church the coming of the Lord was their blessed hope, especially when the church was in persecution. The believers met each other, greeting each other, comforting each other, saying, "The Lord is coming; the Lord is coming."

THE SIGN OF HIS RETURN

Throughout the centuries and the generations the promise of the coming of the Lord is the hope of the church. Generation after generation, believers have been waiting for His return. Even in the first generation they waited for His return. Were they mistaken? No. They were right. Their spirit was right. The more you read the Bible, the more you feel that His coming cannot be too far. Remember, even in the first century, in the book of Revelation chapter 1:3, it says, "The time is near; He is coming." And if it was near in the first century, how much nearer now we are in the twenty-first century. No one knows when He is coming. Our Lord Jesus Himself told us, "No one knows, not even the angels, not even the Son of Man; the Father alone knows." Even though no one knows, one thing is sure; He is coming. He gave us signs to indicate how close is His coming. For instance, the Lord said, "Look at the fig tree. When it begins to bud and to have leaves, you know the summer is near. So when you see these things, you know it is near, at the doors."

At the end of our Lord's ministry, He came to a fig tree full of leaves. He thought there must be fruit, but there was none, nothing to satisfy the longing of His heart. He cursed it, and it dried up, withered, and died. Why? It is because the fig tree is a symbol of the Jewish nation. He had come to work upon that nation for three years and a half, and they produced no fruit, only leaves. It was a big show but no reality; satisfying to man, but utterly unsatisfying to God. The Jewish nation was set aside, as if dead, for almost two thousand years. But the Lord said, "Look, when you see the fig tree begin to bud and to produce leaves, the summer is near. When you see these things happening, you know it is near. He is near at the door."

In 1948, after almost two thousand years, the Jewish nation came into being. It was the surprise of the world. No race, no nation has ever been revived after so many years without land, without government, and yet it did happen. The summer is near. How near it is. At the doors.

AT THE DOORS

I believe you have to be Oriental to understand this parable because in this country when you are at the door (one door), you open the door and you are inside the house. But in the Orient it was not so. In the Orient there are many courts and door after door. The richer you are the more courts you have. The family lived at the very end, so you do not see the family until you cross all the doors. But as soon as you are at the front door you are near.

Brothers and sisters, the Lord is already at the doors. How close, how near! Suddenly He is there. Will that be a great surprise to you—a pleasant surprise? Without going into details, one thing we are sure—you may read the Scripture—so far as we understand, all the prophecies concerning the coming of the Lord *before* His coming have been fulfilled. There are still prophecies left to be fulfilled, but they will be fulfilled *at* the coming of the Lord and *after* the coming of the Lord. But everything that is before the coming of the Lord has been fulfilled. That is to say, the Lord can come at any time.

THE EVENTS OF HIS PRESENCE

The problem with God's people today is because we do not have a real understanding of the meaning of the coming of the Lord. The Bible uses different words to describe His coming, but one word that is used often and is used here in Matthew 24 for "coming" is the Greek word *parousia*. And the word *parousia* means "presence." Today, the Lord is absent, physically speaking. Of course, we know that He is with us in Spirit, but physically speaking, He is absent. But one day He will be present physically. And those who understand Greek tell us this word *parousia*, *presence* is a word that covers a period of time, including a series of events. In other words, the word *presence* has a beginning and has an end. It is not just something that happens suddenly, immediately, once, and it is over. No. It covers a period of time, but that time must be short, and it has a series of events happening during His presence. Now let us try to explain it.

You remember the two men in white in Acts 1:11: "Men of Galilee, why do you look up? He who is taken up (The word *taken up* means "received."), received up, He will return, come back in like manner, in the same way." So His presence is in two parts, just as His departure was in two parts. When He departed from this world, from the Mount of Olives to the cloud—visible; from the cloud to the throne—invisible. Therefore, when He shall come back and return, it will be in the same way: from the throne to the cloud—invisible; from the cloud to the Mount of Olives—visible. That is the reason why there are two different signs being given. One is the sign of a thief. When the Lord shall come, He shall come like a thief. Why? Because He will come quietly, hiddenly, suddenly. He comes and He leaves. But when the thief comes, what will he take? He will take your treasure; he will leave your garbage. And that is exactly what will happen. When the Lord used that kind of metaphor, it is clear that He wants to show us that His presence from the throne to the cloud is invisible, like a thief. A thief will never blow a trumpet saying, "I am coming!" For the Lord to come from the throne to the clouds, He will be like a thief coming. No one knows when. At the hour that you think not, He comes, and when he comes, He steals away the treasure of His heart.

Then two women will be grinding; one is taken, received; one is left. Two men will be working in the field; one is taken, one is left. Two men are sleeping; one is taken, one is left. Now remember, when the Lord said these things, He refers to the church, not to unbelievers. He refers to those who are still living at the coming of the Lord. We are still living. We may have the privilege of being raptured, taken without going through death.

THE MAN CHILD

You remember in Revelation 12, John saw a vision of a woman in travail and a red dragon waiting there. That dragon is not concerned with the woman at that time, but he is deeply concerned with the man child in the womb of that woman. He is waiting there trying to swallow that man child, but the Bible says that as the man child is born, he is taken right to the throne. This man child is what God is looking for. The church is supposed to be the overcoming church, but unfortunately, God's people do not fulfill what God has purposed. Therefore, out of the travail of the church through the ages, God is looking for a man child, the overcomers.

The overcomers are not some special ones; the overcomers are the normal Christians. They follow the Lamb wheresoever He goes. They will be taken because they are the treasure to the Lord. But believers beware, if we are not watchful, if we are laden with eating and drinking and the cares of this life, we may be so rooted to the world we cannot be taken away and are left behind. This "taken" is taken to the throne. They are the welcoming party for the beginning of the presence of the Lord. And immediately after the man child is taken to the throne in Revelation 12 there will be war in the clouds in the air. Michael and his angels will come and fight with Satan and his angels, and there will be no place for Satan because the air is his headquarters. He will be thrown from the air to the earth. The air will be cleared. Why? For the Lord to descend.

Brothers and sisters, it is going to happen. Suddenly, anytime, today may it be so. Suddenly, all over the world some will disappear. Blessed are those who are taken. They are ready; spiritually ready. He will come like a thief. At the time that you think not, He comes and steals away the treasure of His heart.

Then, when Satan is thrown upon this earth, what will happen but the Great Tribulation. Unfortunately, many Christians will still go through that Great Tribulation. In one sense it will be difficult because it will be a great Tribulation that the world has never known before. We have seen enough, but no, there will be the Great Tribulation that we have never seen before. But thank God, God gives us another chance. Even those who fail Him will be given another chance.

People will say, "Christ is here; Christ is there." Don't listen to it because His coming is like lightning. It flashes from the east to the west. The whole world will see it. He will come with the trumpet sound, with the angels. In the twinkling of an eye, those who are dead in Christ will be raised and those who remain and still live will be changed. And all will be caught up to the air—not to the throne, to the air.

Every time I sing hymns singing that our blessed hope is when the trumpet sounds and we shall be taken to the air, I feel, "Too late! Too late! Too late!" How much better, as the Bible says, "Because you keep the word of My patience I will take you away from the time of the tribulation that will come upon this whole world." How much better is that! And that is true. That is the second part of *parousia*. His feet will come upon the Mount of Olives. Mount Olive will be divided into two and the Jewish people, His chosen people will see Him and repent, and He will come to deliver them.

Dear brothers and sisters, don't you think it is time that we wake up? What will happen if He returns? What will happen when we as believers, as the church, are all gathered in the air to meet the Lord in the air? What will be going on in the air while the seven vials, the wrath of God is poured upon this earth? The Bible tells us: "The judgment seat of Christ."

THE JUDGMENT SEAT

Thank God, because our Lord was judged for our sins on Calvary's cross, we will not be judged anymore for life or death, for eternal life or eternal death at the great White Throne of God. In other words, judicial judgment was passed. He has saved us out of judgment, out of death into eternal life. Thank God for that. But that does not mean believers will not be judged. There will be a judgment seat of Christ. It is called a judgment seat. It is not a throne because throne is judicial and it determines life or death, eternal life or eternal death, but it is a seat, *bema*.

What does *bema* mean? Again you find it in the Oriental background. In the Orient you have big families, and in the big family you have the head of the family. It may be a grandfather or a great-grandfather, and as the head of the family he has authority over the whole family. Once in a while there will be a family gathering, and only members of the family can attend. They will gather in a room and in one part of the room

27

there will be an uplifted platform. The head of the family will sit there and there he will judge the members of the family. Those who have done something that adds glory to the family will be recommended and rewarded, and those who have brought shame to the family will be punished, chastised, disciplined. That is *bema*.

Romans 14:10 and II Corinthians 5:10 speak of the judgment of Christ, the judgment seat of God. His family will gather around our Lord Jesus and will be judged according to all that we have done, not before we are saved but after we are saved and receive His life. How do we live before Him?

Brothers and sisters, to those who are ready it is the most blessed time. It is the time that all tears will be wiped away. It is a time that all misunderstanding will be cleared up. It is the time that the cross you have borne through the years will turn to be a crown. How the apostle Paul looked forward to that day! But to those who are not ready it is a time to be feared. That is why we *must* be ready, spiritually ready. It is not an outward, physical readiness. Through the years there are instances where people prophesied, "Christ is coming today or tomorrow or on a certain date," and people left their homes, went to the wilderness clothed in white, waiting for His return. He didn't. It is not physical. Do not be afraid to go to sleep tonight. Do not give up work and stop working, thinking, "Because the Lord is coming, why do I work? How can I sleep?" Readiness is not in these things. In your spirit, in your heart, are you spiritually ready for the coming of the Lord?

Oh Lord, make us ready, not just for fear, but for love's sake. We want You back. We ask in Thy precious name. Amen.

HOW CAN WE BE READY?

Thank God we just had the Lord's Table, and our Lord Jesus said to us: "Do this in remembrance of Me; exhibit His death before the world until I come." So dear brothers and sisters, the Lord has given us one of the best ways to prepare spiritually for His return, and it is remembering Him at His table. We will remember Him until He comes, and the very fact of remembering Him is the best preparation for the coming of the Lord. The Lord knows our weakness, how easily we may forget, how easily we may be enticed away from Him, and that is why it makes us unready for His return. He knows it, and that is the reason why He asks us to remember Him until He comes lest we forget. So thank God for giving us such opportunity of remembering Him at the table, and as we remember Him we are touched, melted by His love. No matter how unlovely we are, He still loves us. He loves us to the very end, to the uttermost, and this love prepares us for His return.

I recall when brother Darby and some of his colleagues were translating the Bible, that they used all kinds of ancient manuscripts. They had to use lots of mental exercise, and they were afraid lest in translating and doing all these mental exercises that their hearts would be led astray from the Lord. And the way to keep them focused on the Lord was to remember Him. So they broke bread every day just to help them to have their hearts filled by the Lord and not their minds filled even with doing something for the Lord.

So we thank God for the privilege we have of coming together, at least once a week, at the Table, remembering how His body was broken for us, given to us, and how His blood was shed for us. Thank God for His unceasing love towards us. May His Spirit keep us until we see Him face to face.

Matthew 24:44—25:1—Wherefore ye also, be ye ready, for in that hour that ye think not the Son of man comes. Who then is the faithful and prudent bondman whom his lord has set over his household, to give them food in season? Blessed is that bondman whom his lord on coming shall find doing thus. Verily I say unto you, that he will set him over all his substance. But if that evil bondman should say in his heart, My lord delays to come, and begin to beat his fellow-bondmen, and eat and drink with the drunken; the lord of that bondman shall come in a day when he does not expect it, and in an hour he knows not of, and shall cut him in two and appoint his portion with the hypocrites: there shall be the weeping and the gnashing of teeth. Then shall the kingdom of the heavens be made like to ten virgins that having taken their torches, went forth to meet the bridegroom.

Shall we pray:

Dear Lord, we want to thank Thee because Thou does love us so much that Thou wants to come back to receive us to Thyself. Oh Lord, we thank Thee for giving us this opportunity to gather before Thee. Open our hearts to Thee; enable Thy Spirit to prepare us for Thy return. Oh Lord, give us such a longing, a yearning for

Thyself that will draw You, as it were, to come back. Oh Lord, how long should we wait? Come quickly, Lord Jesus. Amen.

The theme of this time is: "Spiritual Readiness." We have addressed the first question: Why should there be spiritual readiness? Ready for what? And it is very simple. Spiritual readiness is to be ready spiritually to meet the Lord at His return. We are going to meet Him. He is coming back, but are we prepared? Are we ready to see Him? If you have an appointment with the President of the United States, you do not just go to meet him casually. You prepare because you are not going to meet a common person. How much more do we need to be prepared since we are going to meet the King of kings and the Lord of lords, our Savior, our Master, our Lord, our Lover. In order to meet Him, we need to be prepared, to be ready spiritually.

THE LORD WILL RETURN

We mentioned a little bit about the sureness, the certainty of the return of our Lord. It is because He told us Himself and His apostles told

34

us that our Lord will come back. There are many signs around us telling us that His coming is imminent. Our Lord Himself said, "When you see the fig tree bud and begin to have leaves, you know the summer is near. When you see all these things, you know that it is near, at the doors." So there is no doubt that our Lord Jesus is at the doors, but we do not know which door it is. We only know it is near, very near; nearer probably than any one of us may think because the Lord said, "In the hour that you know not ...." You think that He is not coming yet; it is too early, and suddenly He is there.

We mentioned also that the coming of the Lord is a term that we need to understand. The word used is *parousia* which means "presence," and this word "the presence of the Lord" refers to His physical presence. Thank God that our Lord Jesus, even before He left us, told us He would come in His Spirit. And He has been with us, never leaving us nor forsaking us. He will be with us to the end of the age. He is with us spiritually, but He promised that He would come in person, physically. So His presence is near.

As the two men in white said to the early disciples as they looked at the Lord ascending, "Men of Galilee, why are you looking up? The One who is taken up will come back in like manner, in the same way." So we mentioned that the way He departed was in two stages, from the Mount of Olives to the cloud—visible; then from the cloud to the throne—invisible. When His presence shall come, it will be just the reverse order. From the throne to the cloud will be invisible; He will come as a thief without our knowledge. Suddenly He comes; He takes what is treasure to His heart and He disappears— invisible. But then the second part of His presence will be from the cloud to the Mount of Olives and that is the song we just sang, "Maranatha," when His feet shall touch the Mount of Olives. That is the appearing of His coming, and this is visible as the lightning that shines from the east to the west, and the whole world sees it. He shall come from the cloud with His saints, and He shall come to judge the world. So what we are waiting for is not from the cloud to the Mount of Olives; that is for the world. What we as believers are waiting for is from the throne to the cloud.

THE OVERCOMERS

We find in Revelation 12 the man child. As soon as he is born he is taken to the throne. The dragon waits in vain. This man child represents the overcomers of the church. As we said, the church itself is an overcoming church, but unfortunately, because God's people are defeated, there will be those by the grace of God who are faithful and they shall be the welcoming party to the presence of the Lord. They shall go through the air, the headquarters of the enemy. They have overcome through our Lord Jesus, and they will reach the throne, opening the way, as it were, for the Lord to come from the throne to the cloud. Then Satan will have no place in the air. He will be thrown down upon this earth and there will be the greatest tribulation that the world has ever known. But thank God, even those who are left behind are given a second chance to be faithful, even unto death.

And then, as the Bible says, the trumpet will sound. In the twinkling of an eye the dead in Christ shall be raised, and those who live and remain shall be changed and all shall be taken up to the cloud to meet the Lord who has descended to the cloud (see I Thessalonians 4). And in the air there will be the gathering of all the saints throughout the ages. There will be the judgment seat of Christ, a family judgment, to decide who is to be recommended and rewarded with the kingdom and who will be disciplined during that time.

So it is very, very essential that we be prepared to meet the Lord. We find in the writings of the apostle Paul that this is the day that he was always looking forward to, the day of Christ, that he shall appear before his Lord blameless. May it be so with every one of us.

OUR ATTITUDE CONCERNING HIS COMING

We would like to continue on with the second question: How should we be ready spiritually? We know we need to be ready, but how? We have a real problem before us because we do not know exactly when He will come. If we knew exactly when He shall come, then it is easy to prepare. Why? If it is five years later, we have five more years. Usually we try to prepare at the last minute because that is the way we are. But fortunately, our Lord said, "No one knows the hour or the day—not even the angels." Even the Son of Man while He was on earth said, "Only the Father knows." So we do not know exactly when He will come. He only warns us that when we know not of, when we are unaware, and strangely, when we are unprepared, He comes. So how should we be ready for something that will happen we not know when? Here is the foolishness of man's wisdom. Because we do not know when He will come, we only are warned that when He comes it will be sudden, it will be at the time that probably most people are unaware of, thinking that this cannot be the time, but strangely, God's timing is different. So how can we be prepared?

EVER READY—NEVER READY

Brothers and sisters, do you see the wisdom of God there, that He wants us to be ever ready? No matter when He shall come, we are ready for Him. If the master of the house knew when the thief would come, then he would be ready and would not allow the thief to come unaware. In the same manner, we do not know exactly when

He will come. We only know it is near, at the doors, very close; it can happen anytime, suddenly. So that means we have to be ready all the time. It is not just a matter of being ready once; it is a readiness every day, every hour, every moment. Now if we are ever ready, then no matter when He shall return, we are ready for Him. We should be ever ready but never ready.

If we think we are now ready, most likely we are not ready because we cannot measure the requirement according to our thinking. We have to measure the requirement of readiness according to His thinking. So we may think we are ready but we are not ready, and very often when we think we are ready, this is the time that we relax, sit back, self-confident, and this is the most dangerous time. So I think the secret is to be always ready but never ready. That is the secret. That is the attitude we should take. We should be ready all the time, be vigilant, watchful, in prayer, waiting, and ready for Him. At the same time, we have to trust and depend upon the grace of God because we know our frailty. There is no pride or boasting. If we boast we fail. So we need to be kept in constant humility, casting ourselves upon the longsuffering of God, having no confidence in the flesh, but our confidence is in Christ Jesus. That is the way to be prepared.

SYMPTOMS OF THE DAYS OF NOAH

In the Olivet discourse, our Lord Jesus told us that as in the days of Noah so shall be the coming of the Son of Man. What are the symptoms of the days of Noah? The Lord tells us that in the days of Noah, the people were eating and drinking, marrying and giving in marriage, and suddenly the flood came. There is nothing wrong with eating or drinking, marrying or giving in marriage. These are the things ordained by God. God gave us a body and He prepared food for us. We need to drink; we need to eat, and God's intention is for the family. We need to marry and get married. What is wrong with that? But when eating and drinking, marrying and giving in marriage become the very purpose of life, that is absolutely wrong. We are here not for eating, nor for drinking, not for marrying, nor to be given in marriage; we are here to do the will of God, to glorify Him. That is our purpose.

Dear brothers and sisters, look at the world today. How people make eating and drinking, marrying and giving in marriage—all these legitimate things, illegitimate. They make these as the purpose of life. They live for their belly. Their belly is their God. They live for comfort, for the cares of this life. They live for their own satisfaction, the satisfaction of their flesh, and that is the sign of the last age. Unfortunately, many believers are no different from the people of the world.

What is the purpose of your life? What do you live for? What are the things that really satisfy you? What are the things that you are really seeking? Are you seeking after the world, the things of the world? Or are you seeking after God and after His will? What is the purpose of your life?

THE FAITHFUL BONDMAN

So the Lord said, "Watch, for you know not when the Son of Man shall come. Be ready, because at the time you are unaware of, He suddenly comes." Then He began to speak a parable: Who is the prudent and faithful bondman that his lord, when he goes away, commits his household to that servant? And if that servant is prudent, wise, and faithful, he will give food to the household in season because he knows the mind of the master and he is faithful to what the master has entrusted to him. Then, when the master shall return, he shall give him all the substance of his house. But if the same person (The Lord is not telling us about two different people, one wise, one foolish; the Lord is saying to us that you can be wise or you can be foolish.) is the evil servant, thinking that the Lord delays, He will not come back that soon, and he begins to eat and drink and get drunk and even beat his fellow bondmen, then at the time that he is unaware the master returns. And when the master returns, he will cut him in two and will put him in the same class as a hypocrite, and there will be the gnashing of teeth and weeping.

We are His bondmen. A bondman is more than just a servant of today. A bondman in the old days was a slave; he was bought by the master. He owned nothing, not even his own life. He had no rights of any kind. He belonged to his master. And we as believers are all bondmen of

God because our Lord has bought us with a price. What a price He has paid for such worthless people such as we are! He gave His very life; He shed His very blood. He bought us for Himself. He entrusted His household to us, the family of God, the church of God. He wants us to be faithful and prudent, not to be foolish and unfaithful. The only difference that makes us either prudent and faithful or evil depends upon one thing. What is your attitude towards the coming of the Lord? If you think that the Lord is coming soon, that He can return at any moment, then you will be wise and faithful in everything. Every day you will be diligently doing His bidding because He may come at any moment and you want to be ready.

THE EVIL SERVANT

But the evil servant said in his heart, "The Lord delays His return." He does not think the Lord will return so soon. There is plenty of time to enjoy himself, and maybe at the last moment he will repent and then he will prepare. He thinks he is wise to get the two worlds, but he is the foolish one because the master will come at the time he is not aware of. Sometimes when we are preaching the gospel to people, they say, "Yes, we know we need a Savior. At my deathbed I will repent." But are you sure that at your deathbed you will repent? How many people die suddenly! That is the foolishness of man's wisdom. This servant thought there was plenty of time to enjoy the world first. As people say, "When I am as old as you are then I will seek heavenly things." Brothers and sisters, that will be too late!

How do we prepare for the coming of the Lord when we do not know exactly when He will arrive? It depends mainly upon our attitude. What is your attitude towards His coming? Are you expecting Him any moment? Are you saying in your heart, "He delays; He will not come now. Maybe He will come tomorrow but certainly not today." What is your attitude towards the coming of the Lord? We need to place ourselves under the light of God and allow His light to shine upon us because only in His light do we see light. Our heart is deceitful above all things, so deceitful that it deceives even ourselves. We need constantly to pray the prayer of David in

Psalm 139: "Search me and know my heart. Examine me and know my mind. See if there is any evil, grievous, idolatrous thing in me." Let His light search every one of us. Am I a prudent and faithful bondman or am I an evil bondman? It is my attitude, my heart attitude.

What do you think about the coming of the Lord? Do you really believe? Do you really think that He may come at this moment? Do you think, "Oh no, not today; maybe 2040 or 2060." The famous scientist, Isaac Newton, actually wrote more spiritual books than scientific books, and he tried to estimate when the Lord would return. He was a mathematician. And in his estimate it will be 2060. Foolishness!

Brothers and sisters, we do not know when He is coming. We only know He can come at any moment. What is our attitude?

A LIFE PLEASING TO THE LORD

Then our Lord Jesus followed with two other parables. In what respect, in what areas should we be ready? When the Lord returns, He will reckon with us. Whatever was covered by the blood of the Lord Jesus in the past will not be remembered anymore. But after we have believed in the Lord Jesus, after we have received His life, how do we live our days? How do we serve Him in our work? We will have to give an account for these things. Therefore our preparation should be twofold. We need to prepare for a life that will be pleasing to Him, and we need to prepare for a service that will be acceptable to Him. So for this reason our Lord Jesus followed with two other parables.

THE WITNESS OF THE TWO

First of all, I have to say that I am not trying to give a strict interpretation on what follows because strictly speaking, if you notice, there is a time difference here. In Matthew 24:40 it says, "Then two shall be in the field; one is taken and one is left; two women grinding at the mill, one is taken and one is left. Watch therefore for ye know not in what hour your Lord returns."

The word *then* is indicating a time factor, and according to the context the time factor happens at the beginning of parousia, the beginning of the presence of the Lord. So you have two, and two

47

is a number of witnesses. By the witness of two and three everything will be certain. And here the two represents those believers who are still living at the time of the beginning of parousia, and we are in that hour. So these two refer to living Christians who are living at the time of the beginning of parousia. And how will parousia begin? Then, two will be grinding the mill; that is morning. Two will be working in the field; that is noontime. And two will be sleeping in the bed; that is nighttime. And suddenly, one is taken and one is left. The earth is round, so in some places it is morning, in other places noontime, in some other places it is midnight. Suddenly the Lord comes as a thief, and He will steal away what He considers as treasure of His heart. That is the man child, and they will be taken to the throne to prepare the way of the descending of the Lord from the throne to the cloud.

THE TEN VIRGINS

But when you look at Matthew 25:1 it is another day. The "then" here is a little bit different time-wise. He said, "Then shall the kingdom of the heavens be made like to ten virgins that having taken their torches, went forth to meet the bridegroom." This is a parable of ten virgins. The Bible uses the word *virgin*, spiritually speaking, in a very specific way. So far as the world is concerned, people are adulterers or adulteresses. Only those who are redeemed by the blood of the Lord Jesus, cleansed by His precious blood, are virgins. In II Corinthians 11 the apostle Paul told the Corinthians, "I offer you to the Lord as chaste virgins; I engage you to Christ, but I am afraid you may be enticed away from the simplicity of Christ."

Brothers and sisters, we are virgins; not only virgins, but engaged. We all are engaged to Christ, and as engaged virgins we need to be chaste virgins. In other words, we need to be prepared for our Bridegroom. We are living for our Bridegroom, waiting for the marriage, keeping ourselves pure, doing things that we know will please Him and not ourselves, and not doing anything that we know will displease Him. We are as chaste virgins engaged to Christ. But how easily we can be enticed! May the Lord have mercy on us.

These ten virgins do not represent unbelievers. Yes, among the ten virgins there are five wise and five foolish. It is just like the two who are living; one is taken, one is left. Strictly speaking, these ten virgins represent the saints throughout the ages. They went out to meet the Lord and the Lord tarried, and they slept. The *sleeping* here is not a spiritual sleeping because the wise virgins slept too. The *sleeping* here is physical death because as believers we go to sleep—we will wake up again; we never die. So strictly speaking, these ten virgins refer to the saints through the ages. They all have torches. In other words, they have oil in the torch. They have the indwelling Holy Spirit that makes them lights of the world. Not only that, they all went out to meet the Bridegroom. Can you think of an unbeliever going out to meet Christ? Never! When we are first saved, we turn away from idols unto God, and naturally we wait for His return. We wait to see Him. Every believer is like that. But the Bridegroom tarried, and they could not wait any longer. They all went to sleep, died. So strictly speaking, these ten virgins speak of the saints of the past who have died.

The number of the church today is seven, but in eternity it is twelve, so you have the ten here and the two there. That makes it twelve. You see the whole picture of the church of God. But we are not trying to be technically correct; we will try to use this and derive from it the spiritual principle that lies behind it. Nothing is mentioned of their spiritual condition, so we do not know why one is taken and one is left. But the reason is given for the virgins. When the wise virgins went out to meet the Bridegroom, they did not know when the Bridegroom would come, so they were well prepared. Not only did they have oil in their torches to make it light but they also carried extra oil in the vessel, just in case the oil was depleted they could add oil to it so it would be burning all the time until the Bridegroom comes. They are wise, and this speaks of being filled with the Holy Spirit.

BE FILLED WITH THE SPIRIT

Brothers and sisters, every believer has the Holy Spirit. We are not only born of the Spirit, but the Holy Spirit comes and dwells in our spirit and together we cry out, "Abba, Father" to

God. So every believer has the Holy Spirit in him or in her. Thank God for that! And the Holy Spirit, who is in us, will never leave us nor forsake us, and it is His work every day to be our constant teacher, teaching us in all things—big things and small things. And we are exhorted to listen and to obey the voice of the Spirit of God within us, and this is the way we grow in the Lord. Everyone has the Holy Spirit but not every believer has extra oil in the vessel. That is to say, not every believer is filled with the Spirit of God.

Ephesians 5:18 says, "Do not be drunk for this is debauchery, but be filled with the Spirit." To be filled with the Spirit is to be constantly filled with the Spirit. To be filled with the Spirit is to be ruled by the Spirit. We have the Holy Spirit, but do we listen to the voice of the Spirit? Do not shut your ear. Listen to the voice of the Spirit. Is the Spirit in control of your life? Are you being filled with the Spirit? It is not just one experience five years ago, but it is daily, hourly, being filled continuously with the Holy Spirit. Let the Holy Spirit rule over your life. Walk in the Spirit, obey the Holy Spirit, live by the Spirit. That is the wise virgin. But the foolish virgins just had oil in their torches. They were not prepared for emergency. They must have vessels too, but they thought they were wise because they filled the vessels with other things, thinking that the other things were more important than the Holy Spirit. Today, as we are living, nobody can tell the difference.

But one day, the voice comes: "Behold, the Bridegroom! The Bridegroom is already here." They all wake up. That is resurrection. That is the fulfillment of I Thessalonians 4:

"The dead in Christ shall be raised and they will all be taken to the air to meet the descended Lord." When that time comes, then what happens? The five wise virgins put extra oil in their torches, and the lights are burning. They are able to meet the Bridegroom and enter into the marriage feast, and the door is shut. The foolish virgins find that their light is going out; it is dimming. So they ask the wise virgins: "Give us some of the oil." But the wise virgins say, "It cannot be done because this is something you have to buy. This is something you have to pay a cost. Go and buy it." But when they go the door is shut.

In other words, some virgins are chaste virgins, walking in the Spirit, filled by the Holy Spirit, but some virgins are foolish. They seek the world, the things of the world just like Luke 21 says, "Do not be laden with eating and drinking and the cares of this life." What a difference!

How can we be filled with the Holy Spirit? Very simple—empty yourself. The more you are emptied, the more you are filled. It is just like the air that fills this room, but because we are all here occupying the space we compress the air; but the air is here. If we move out the air will fill the whole place. The only way to be filled with the Spirit is through emptying, and this is the reason why our Lord said, "Deny yourself, take up your cross, and follow Me." That is the way to empty yourself. The more you empty yourself the more the Spirit will fill you. The more you fill yourself with yourself, the less the Holy Spirit has any place in your life. Very simple.

How do we prepare for the return of the Lord? So far as your life is concerned learn to let the Holy Spirit rule over your life. Let Him fill you; let Him lead you; let Him teach you; let Him guide you; walk by Him; live by Him, because He brings Christ to us, and He brings us to Christ. That is the only way.

At the coming of the Lord the wise virgins have the privilege of being at the wedding feast of the Lamb, but the foolish virgins were shut out of the door. It does not mean that they are not saved; it means they have no part in the kingdom of heaven that comes on this earth. Christ shall rule over this earth with righteousness for a thousand years. What a loss! Now that is the life part.

SERVICE ACCEPTABLE TO THE LORD

This is followed by another parable, the parable of the master. Before he goes away he gives talents, his property, to his bondservants according to their ability. One is given five talents, one is given two talents, and one is given one talent. Then he went away, but one day he is coming back. He will reckon with his servants as to what happened to the talents he had given to them. The one with five talents came and said, "Lord, you gave me five talents. I have trafficked with it according to your will and increased it five more talents." The lord said, "Good and faithful bondman. You are faithful in little things; I am going to entrust you with more things. Come into the joy of the lord." The one with two talents also came and said, "Lord, I have earned two more talents." The lord said the same thing; no difference. But the one with one talent came and he said, "I know you are a hard master; you want to reap where there is no sowing, so I am afraid. I wrapped that talent up in a handkerchief and buried it in the earth. Now here is your talent." And the lord said, "Foolish servant, if you really think that I am a hard master, at least you should give it to a bank and get some interest. Take away the talent that was given to him and give it to the one with ten talents, and this one will be cast out in darkness with gnashing and weeping."

Brothers and sisters, what does it tell us here? It tells us that we who are the Lord's, so far as our life is concerned, we are virgins towards Him, but so far as bondmen are concerned, we are His servants, His bondmen. And He has given us talents, not only spiritual gifts, but even opportunities. Whatever He has entrusted to us we are to be faithfully using for the increase of the kingdom of God. And if we are lazy, we even bury it without losing it, it is still too bad.

So the lesson is that in this lifetime we are all bondservants serving the Lord with what He has entrusted to us, and these things are not for ourselves. It is not ours; it is His, and we are to use what He has entrusted to us for His increase, for His glory. How do we do that? Are we using these to serve our purpose? Or are we using these to serve His purpose? One day there will be a reckoning. So let us understand the heart of our Lord. What He has entrusted to us we are to be faithfully and wisely using for the increase of the kingdom and His righteousness. Then our service will be rewarded. And if we do not, we will have no part in the kingdom age, a thousand years, when the Lord shall rule over this earth, but rather be cast out into outer darkness. We do not lose our eternal salvation— saved—but we are disciplined so that we can be matured.

So brothers and sisters, how are we to be ready? Number one: our attitude towards His coming must be right. Number two: in our life let us be filled with the Spirit, led by the Spirit, and in our service do His bidding faithfully. And thank God, when He shall return, He will preserve us blameless at the coming of the Lord. He who calls us is faithful; He will perform it.

Shall we pray:

Dear Lord, we do thank Thee for telling us that no one knows when Thou art coming. We thank Thee that Thou dost desire that we should be ready every moment, and yet Lord, we feel that we are never ready. We depend on Thee. It is all of grace. Dear Lord, we pray that none of us here will be left behind, but everyone will meet Thee joyfully. We ask in Thy name. Amen.

QUESTIONS & ANSWERS

I have quite a number of questions addressed to me, and it seems to me that these questions are more for information than for life. Hopefully, by the grace of God, with a better understanding it may stir us to seek the Lord more earnestly, and thus be spiritually prepared for His return.

I tried to group all these questions under two headings. One is: "The Relationship between Overcomers and the Kingdom." The other is: "The Relationship between Rapture and the Coming of the Lord." Now these subjects need more conferences because it is impossible to cover these two huge inclusive questions. But I will try to make it very simple, and hopefully it will be clear and a help to us.

THE RELATIONSHIP BETWEEN OVERCOMERS AND THE KINGDOM

There is a definite relationship between overcomers and the kingdom. Of course, when we talk about overcomers, we really refer to the overcomers in the church. In Revelation, chapters 2—3, these letters are addressed to the churches, but at the end of every letter it always says, "He that has an ear to hear, let him hear what the Spirit says to the churches." It is for the churches. "But he that overcomes..." In other words, the whole church is supposed to be full of overcomers, nothing but overcomers. Why? Because our Lord is *the* Overcomer. He overcame, therefore He was worthy to take the scroll, worthy to claim the creation for Himself. And the church, being the body of Christ, should be an overcoming church. By His overcoming we overcome sin, we overcome the world, we overcome Satan, and we even overcome ourselves. That is what we ought to be.

In Luke 12 we are told: "Fear not little flock, it is the good pleasure of the Father to give you the kingdom." And the little flock there refers to the whole church because the church in comparison with the world is like a little flock. So the kingdom is given to the church. The church is supposed to reign with Christ for a thousand years upon this earth, but unfortunately, because the majority in the church are being overcome instead of overcoming, our Lord Jesus calls for overcomers. In other words, He calls them, those who will be faithful to His revelation, faithful to the vision of Christ, those who are normal Christians, those who will follow the Lamb wherever He goes. They do not choose their own way, but they choose to deny themselves, take up their crosses daily and follow the Lord. These are the overcomers of the church. So the overcomers receive the kingdom as a reward from our Lord.

I faintly remember a story, but I may not be exactly accurate. One day John Wesley dreamed a dream, and he dreamed that he went to heaven. At the door he asked the angel: "Who is in heaven? Are there any Episcopalians?"

The angel said, "No."

"Are there any Presbyterians?"

"No."

"Are there any Baptists?"

"No."

"Ah," John Wesley said, "it must be the Methodists." So he asked, "Are there any Methodists?"

And the angel said, "No."

"Then who is in heaven?"

"Those who are redeemed by the precious blood of the Lamb."

In like manner is the kingdom. Who will be in the kingdom of heaven? Who will reign and rule with Christ for a thousand years? Who will be privileged to enter into the joy of the Lord? And who will be given the real service that the bondmen of Christ will perform? The overcomers. It is only based upon those who overcome because they are one with the Head, the Overcomer. So I hope this will lay a foundation for us to really seek earnestly to enter into the kingdom, not only for our sakes, but mostly for the sake of our Lord.

The kingdom of the heavens is to be taken by violence and the violent seize upon it. The violence here is not doing violence to others. How often we do violence to others! The violence here is to be violent to ourselves, denying ourselves. That is doing violence. And the violent seize upon the kingdom. So may the Lord help us.

THE RELATIONSHIP BETWEEN RAPTURE AND THE PRESENCE OF THE LORD

The second heading is "The relationship of rapture and the presence of the Lord." Let me tell you a story first. Once I was in Peru. I was invited to go and meet a couple who were missionaries there, Bert Elliot and his wife, and they loved the Lord. They spent their lives in Peru working in the jungles and on the mountains. Half a year they lived in a little boat sailing in the Amazon River, visiting village after village, and the other half of the time they drove a truck over the mountains, preaching, visiting, and pulling teeth. So I was invited to go there and meet them. They lived in Yurimagua. It is a place that you have to fly into because there is no road into it. While I was there, there was a conference for the natives. The native believers came from all over, walking through the jungles to arrive at the place.

I was leaving the next day, so they asked me if I could speak during that first evening. But before the meeting a missionary from a neighboring village arrived, and we had dinner together. This missionary was very inquisitive. He wanted to find out who I am, what I believe, and where I stand. So he began to ask me question after question, and gradually the questions became more interesting. I knew his background. He was an Exclusive Brethren, and I knew his teaching. So he began to ask me about rapture. I tried to avoid any conflict, so I said, "I believe all believers will be raptured." He said, "How many times?"

Now I did not want to get into controversy, so I told my brother, "Brother, we may hold different interpretations, but we all believe the Bible is the word of God. I happen to believe that the overcomers will be raptured first, those who are still living at the time of the return of the Lord, and then the rest of the church will be raptured."

Do you know what he said? He said, "Brother, you do not believe the Bible."

I said, "Brother, I do believe the Bible, just as you do. But we seem to differ in our interpretation."

He said, "No, you do not believe the Bible."

On the way to the meeting he was murmuring all the time: "If you speak, then I will not speak. If you speak, I will not speak." So I turned to our dear brother Bert and said, "I will not speak because he lives here in the neighborhood, and I am leaving tomorrow." So I refused to speak in that conference.

Now brothers and sisters, I hope we are not like that dear exclusive brother. So far as I understand, the whole church will be raptured, but those who are prepared will go first—two grinding in the morning, two working at midday, and two sleeping in the night. One is taken, one is left.

In the Bible you cannot find the word *rapture*. The word used is *taken, receive up*, but the meaning is *rapture*. So it really depends upon your understanding of the coming of the Lord. Unfortunately, I think in Christianity most seem to hold the view that the coming of the Lord means only the appearing of His coming. That is to say, the coming of the Lord is when He shall come with the cloud, with the trumpet sound, with the angels, and He descends upon the Mount of Olives—one event, one moment. But so far as my understanding is concerned, and so far as those who understand Greek are concerned, we are told that parousia, the presence, covers a period of time and includes a series of events.

As the believers were looking up to the Lord, as His feet left the Mount of Olives going up, He was taken up. They beheld Him. They looked at Him, and then a cloud took Him. They could not see Him anymore, but they were still looking upward, and two men in white appeared: "Men of Galilee, why do you look up? The One who is taken, received up to heaven, will come back in like manner." So to me I feel His departure is in two parts, therefore His presence will also be in two parts. It is just reversed in order. Parousia begins from the throne to the cloud, and it ends from the air to the Mount of Olives. So we do thank the Lord that He is coming back.

Let me put it this way. If what we are waiting for the coming of the Lord is the appearing of the Lord to this world, then we can more or less figure out when He will be coming. Why? He will not come before the beginning of the seven years when the antichrist shall make a pact with the Jewish nation. It will be at the end of the seven years. So we have more than seven years to go yet; sleep on. But because His coming is like a thief, therefore brothers and sisters, we cannot afford to sleep anymore. Just like the apostle Paul says in Romans: "This is the time that we cannot sleep on anymore. Wake up! Put on Christ, because His coming is any time." So far as I am concerned, this seems to help me to be more alert, watchful, waiting before the Lord, than to say that His coming will not be a fact until the trumpet sounds, until the lightning shines from the east to the west, until everybody shall see Him; then He comes. Brothers and sisters, it may be too late.

So I do believe that every Christian, every true believer will be raptured. I believe the whole church will be raptured, but I also believe that those who are prepared and ready will go first. Of course, at the first rapture, only those who are still alive at the coming of the Lord, only those who are still living on this earth and yet their hearts are prepared will be raptured, as the man child in Revelation 12. As you go on you will find, "Rejoice, those who dwell in heaven because Satan has been thrown down upon this earth and they overcome the accuser by the blood of the Lamb, by the word of their testimony, and they loved not their lives even unto death." These are the overcomers. They form the man child, the welcoming party to the return of the Lord. Dear brothers and sisters, by the grace of God only, may we be among the remnant.

What will happen at the coming of the Lord? Of course, this is in the future, so we cannot be a hundred per cent sure and say, "Now it has to follow this order." Our God always surprises us. But so far as we can read from the word of God, it does seem that there is a sequence of events happening. First, suddenly, all over the world some Christians disappear; they are raptured, and this rapture starts the war in the air. Michael and his angels will fight against Satan and his followers and there will be no place for Satan anymore. He will be cast down upon the earth. In other words, the air is clear, and then our Lord will come from the throne to the air with those overcomers.

During that period, because Satan is now on earth, what can you expect but the Great Tribulation? a tribulation that has never happened in the world before, something beyond our comprehension—terrible. During that Great Tribulation two kinds of people will suffer most—the Jews and the Christians who remain on earth, because every one is to have the mark of the beast upon them. Without that they cannot trade, they have nothing to eat, they will be killed, persecuted.

Because the Jews believe in one God, they will not bow to the image of the beast. But thank God, God prepared them for being faithful. You remember in Revelation the two messengers sent to them. I believe one will be Moses and the other will be Elijah, and they will testify, strengthen those faithful Jews going through Jacob's trouble. They were the one hundred and forty-four thousand of the tribes of Israel sealed with the seal of the living God. God will protect them through Jacob's trouble.

In like manner, among the saints many wake up and are willing to die for the Lord. God gives them another opportunity. And the heat of the persecution ripens God's people, so there comes the harvest. You remember in Revelation 14 there is a man with a golden sickle sitting on the cloud. That is our Lord, and He throws down the sickle and harvests His harvest. That is the fulfillment of I Thessalonians 4. Those who are dead in Christ will be raised from the dead, and those who are living and still remain will be changed, and all will be raptured, caught up to the air to meet the Lord. The whole church will be raptured.

What will happen upon this earth? No Christians anymore, nothing but the wrath of God, the seven vials, the wrath of God poured upon this earth. The judgment of the world has come.

What happens in the air? The judgment seat of Christ. We will all be gathered as the family of

God in the presence of our elder brother, who will judge us according to what we do, how we live after we become members of the family. And those who overcome will be rewarded with the kingdom, but those who fail will be disciplined. That is all we know; cast into outer darkness. We do not know what outer darkness means. We are told that in the early days when the king had a marriage feast for his son, the whole place would be lit up, but outside the compound there would be darkness. In other words, the foolish virgins will be barred from enjoying the marriage feast. They will be outside. The wicked servant will be cast into outer darkness, that is outside of the kingdom, and there will continue the blessed work of discipline until they too are matured.

God's purpose cannot be defeated. We may delay His purpose but never defeat His purpose. If we are not transformed through discipline during this world to be conformed to the image of Christ, then during the kingdom age we will be given another opportunity. It is the will of God that whom He has known, He has called, and whom he has called He has justified, and whom He has justified, He has glorified. Thank God, this is our assurance. Eventually, all who are called, chosen will be like Christ, and then we will be with Him in that eternal home in eternity.

At the end of the Great Tribulation there will be the last war. Christ will come from the cloud with His overcoming saints. He will ride on a white horse, and those who follow Him are the chosen ones. His feet will come upon the Mount of Olives. The Mount of Olives will be split in two and those faithful Jews who have not been killed will flee through that gap. They saw the Lord; they repented; they turned to Him (Zechariah 12—14). And Christ and His overcomers will fight the last war, the war of Armageddon. And after that there will be the judgment of the nations (Matthew 25:31-46), and then the kingdom.

So roughly, that is the general outline that we seem to be able to find out from the word of God, but exactly how it will happen nobody knows. I dare not to be a false prophet. God have mercy on me.

So dear brothers and sisters, in a general sense it will give you some idea, and hopefully this will inspire us to really seek the Lord, give ourselves absolutely, totally to the Lord; no reservation, nothing held back. May the Lord help us.

Other Books Printed By
Christian Testimony Ministry

SPEAKER	TITLE
DANA CONGDON	MARRIAGE, SINGLENESS, AND THE WILL OF GOD
	RECOVERY & RESTORATION
	THE HOLY SPIRIT
	HEBREWS
A.J. FLACK	TENT OF HIS SPLENDOUR
STEPHEN KAUNG	ACTS
	BE YE THEREFORE PERFECT
	CALLED OUT UNTO CHRIST
	CALLED TO THE FELLOWSHIP OF GOD'S SON
	DIVINE LIFE AND ORDER
	FOR ME TO LIVE IS CHRIST
	GLORIOUS LIBERTY OF THE CHILDREN OF GOD
	GOD'S PURPOSE FOR THE FAMILY
	I WILL BUILD MY CHURCH
	MEDITATIONS ON THE KINGDOM
	RECOVERY
	SPIRITUAL EXERCISE
	SPIRITUAL LIFE (II CORINTHIANS SERIES)
	TEACH US TO PRAY
	THE CROSS
	THE FULNESS OF CHRIST—IN THE BOOK OF REVELATION
	THE HEADSHIP OF CHRIST
	THE KINGDOM AND THE CHURCH
	THE KINGDOM OF GOD
	THE LAST CALL TO THE CHURCHES, THE CALL TO OVERCOME
	THE LIFE OF OUR LORD JESUS
	THE LIFE OF THE CHURCH, THE BODY OF CHRIST
	THE LORD'S TABLE
	TWO GUIDEPOSTS FOR INHERITING THE KINGDOM
	VISION OF CHRIST (REVELATION)
	WHO ARE WE?

Why Do We So Gather?
Worship

Lance Lambert
Called Unto His Eternal Glory
God's Eternal Purpose
In the Day of Thy Power
Jacob I Have Loved
Living Faith
Lessons from the Life of Moses
Love Divine
My House Shall be a House of Prayer
Preparation for the Coming of the Lord
Reigning with Christ
Spiritual Character
The Gospel of the Kingdom
The Importance of Covering
The Last Days and God's Priorities
The Prize
The Supremacy of Jesus Christ
Thine is the Power!
Thou Art Mine

T. Austin-Sparks
The Lord's Testimony and the World Need

Harvey Cedars Conference

Stephen Kaung
Heavenly Vision
Spiritual Responsibility

Congdon, Hile, Kaung
Spiritual Ministry
Spiritual Authority
Spiritual House
Spiritual Submission

Stephen Kaung
Spiritual Knowledge
Spiritual Power
Spiritual Reality
Spiritual Value
Spiritual Blessing
Spiritual Discernment

Spiritual Warfare
Spiritual Ascendancy
Spiritual Mindedness
Spiritual Perfection
Spiritual Fulness
Spiritual Sonship
Spiritual Stewardship
Spiritual Travail
Spiritual Inheritance
Harvey Cedars Conference:
Hile, Kaung, Lambert
The King is Coming